Birds in Origami

John Montroll

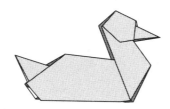

Dover Publications, Inc.
New York

To Heidi, Gene and Glenn

Bibliographical Note

Birds in Origami is a new work, first published by
Dover Publications, Inc., in 1995.

Library of Congress Cataloging-in-Publication Data

Montroll, John.
  Birds in origami / John Montroll.
    p. cm.
  ISBN-13: 978-0-486-28341-8 (pbk.)
  ISBN-10: 0-486-28341-0 (pbk.)
    1. Origami. 2. Birds in art. I. Title.
TT870.M552 1994
736'.982—dc20

94-40618

Manufactured in the United States by Courier Corporation
28341016   2013
www.doverpublications.com

Introduction

This book presents a collection of original origami birds, which you might find in a pond, over the sea, or in a tropical rain forest. You might even find some in your own backyard.

The models are arranged in order of skill level, from the simple-to-fold duck to the high-intermediate parrot.

The diagrams follow the internationally approved Randlett–Yoshizawa style, which is easy to follow once you have learned the basic folds. You can use any kind of square paper for these models, but the best results and most precise folding can be achieved using standard origami paper, which is colored on one side and white on the other. In these diagrams, the shading represents the colored side. Origami paper can be found in many hobby shops or purchased by mail from Origami USA, a nonprofit organization of dedicated paperfolders. For more information about the group, send a self-addressed business-size envelope with two first-class stamps to:

> Origami USA
> 15 West 77th St.
> New York, NY 10024–5192

Origami paper, and a catalog of other available craft books, can also be ordered from Dover Publications, Inc., at:

> Dover Publications, Inc.
> 31 East 2nd St.
> Mineola, NY 11501

Enjoy, and Happy Folding.

John Montroll

Symbols

Lines

— — — — — — — — — Valley fold, fold in front.

—·—·—·—·—·—·— Mountain fold, fold behind.

———————————— Crease line.

····························· X-ray or guide line.

Arrows

 Fold in this direction.

Fold behind.

Unfold.

Fold and unfold.

Turn over.

Sink or three dimensional folding.

Place your finger between these layers.

Basic Folds

Rabbit Ear.

To fold a rabbit ear, one corner is folded in half and laid down to a side.

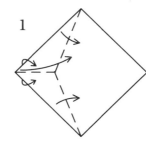

1

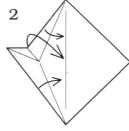

2

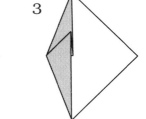

3

Fold a rabbit ear.

A three-dimensional intermediate step.

Double Rabbit Ear.

If you were to bend a straw you would be folding the double rabbit ear.

1

2

(Straw)

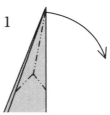

1

2

Make a double rabbit ear.

Squash Fold.

In a squash fold, some paper is opened and then made flat. The shaded arrow shows where to place your finger.

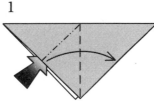

1

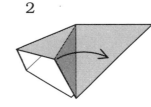

2

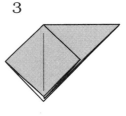

3

Squash-fold.

A three-dimensional intermediate step.

Petal Fold.

In a petal fold, one point is folded up while two opposite sides meet each other.

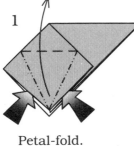

1

2

3

Petal-fold.

A three-dimensional intermediate step.

Inside Reverse Fold.

In an inside reverse fold, some paper is folded between layers. Here are two examples.

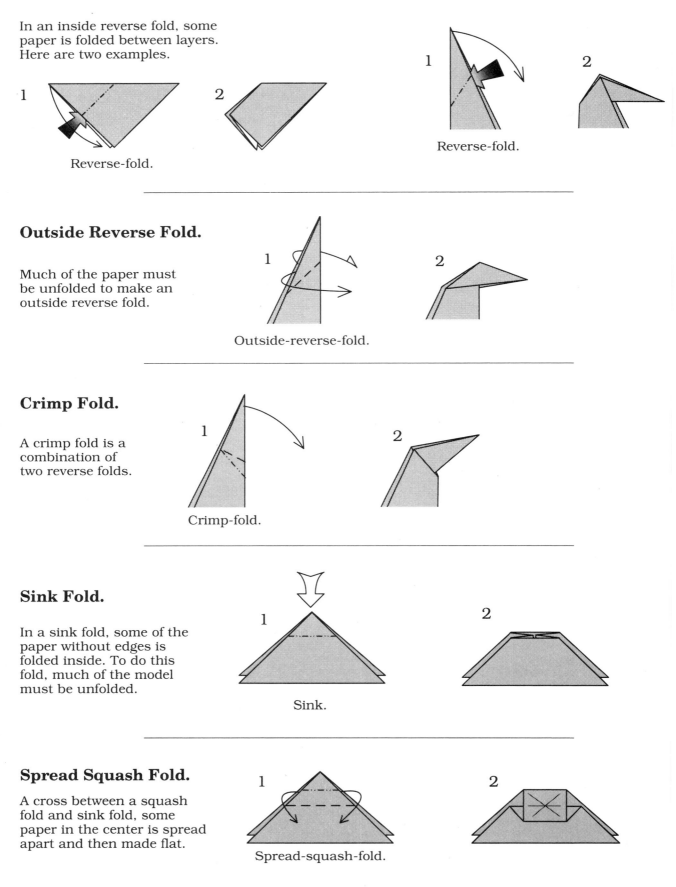

Reverse-fold.

Reverse-fold.

Outside Reverse Fold.

Much of the paper must be unfolded to make an outside reverse fold.

Outside-reverse-fold.

Crimp Fold.

A crimp fold is a combination of two reverse folds.

Crimp-fold.

Sink Fold.

In a sink fold, some of the paper without edges is folded inside. To do this fold, much of the model must be unfolded.

Sink.

Spread Squash Fold.

A cross between a squash fold and sink fold, some paper in the center is spread apart and then made flat.

Spread-squash-fold.

6

Contents

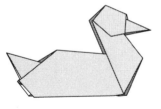

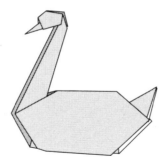

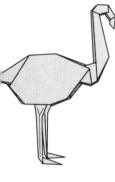

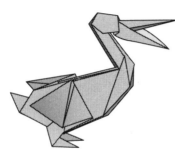

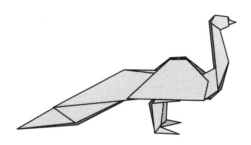

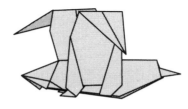

Hummingbird
Page 27

Cardinal
Page 30

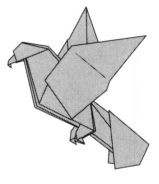

Cormorant
Page 33

Stork
Page 36

Eagle
Page 39

Canary
Page 42

Parrot
Page 45

Duck

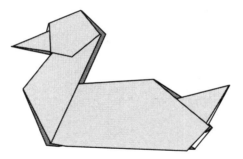

1

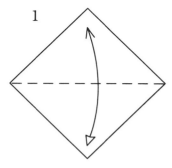

Fold and unfold.

2

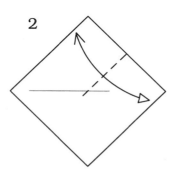

Fold and unfold.

3

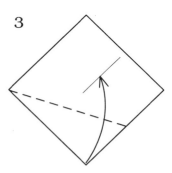

Fold the corner
to the center line.

4

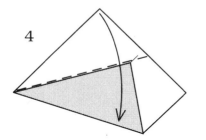

5

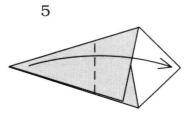

6

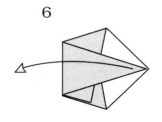

Unfold.

7

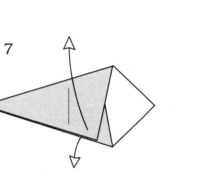

Fold and unfold.

8

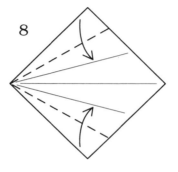

9

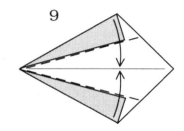

10

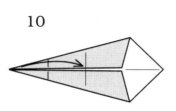

Fold to the center line.

11

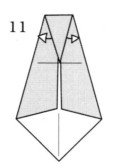

Pull out from inside.

12

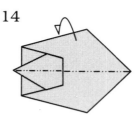

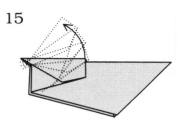

13

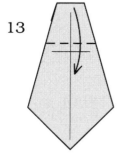

Fold down from above the center line and rotate.

14

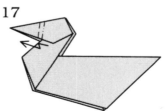

Fold behind.

15

Slide the neck.

16

Slide the head.

17

Fold the tip in and out for the beak.

18

Fold in and out for the tail.

19

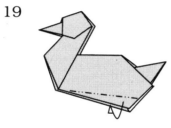

Fold a thin layer behind, repeat behind.

20

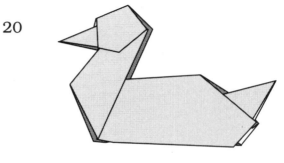

Duck

Swan

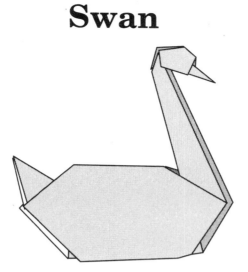

1

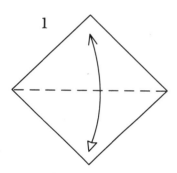

Fold and unfold.

2

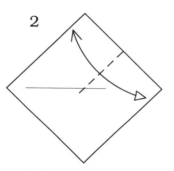

Fold and unfold.

3

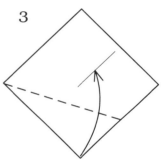

Fold the corner
to the center line.

4

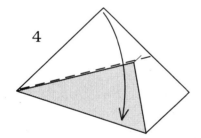

5

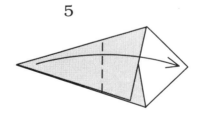

6

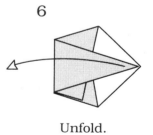

Unfold.

7

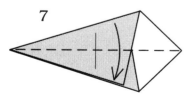

8

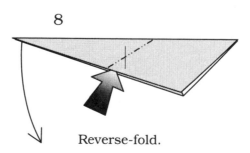

Reverse-fold.

9

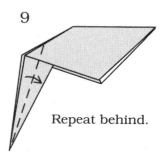

Repeat behind.

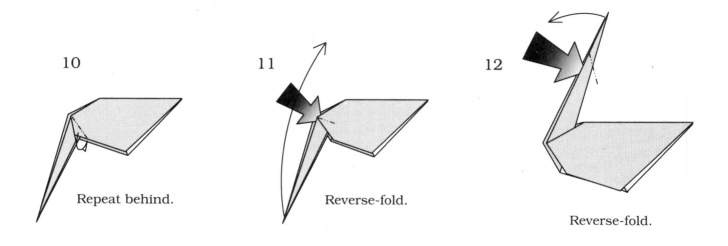

10

Repeat behind.

11

Reverse-fold.

12

Reverse-fold.

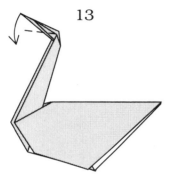

13

Spread the head
while folding down.

14

Fold the beak in and out.

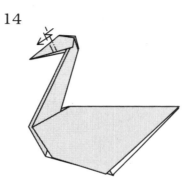

15

Fold the tail in and out.

16

Fold a thin layer
behind, repeat behind.

17

Swan

Goose

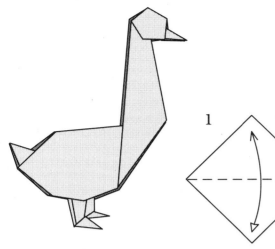

1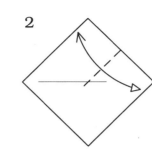

Fold and unfold.

2

Fold one corner to
the other and unfold.

3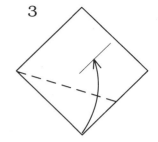

Fold the corner
to the center line.

4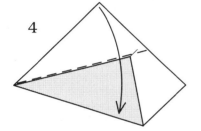

5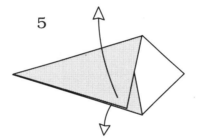

Unfold.

6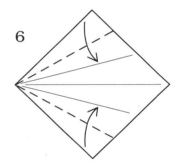

Fold to the creases.

7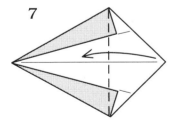

8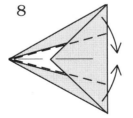

9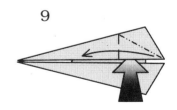

Squash-fold.

10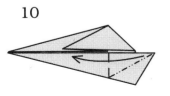

Squash-fold.

11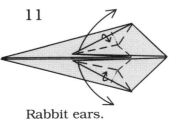

Rabbit ears.

12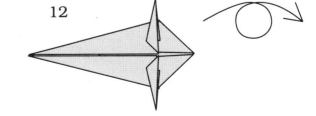

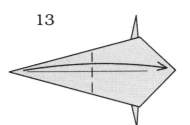

13

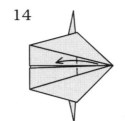

14

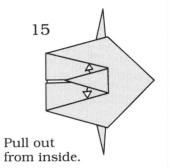

15

Pull out
from inside.

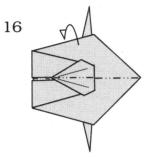

16

Fold behind.

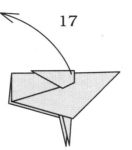

17

Slide the neck.

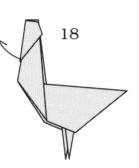

18

Slide the head.

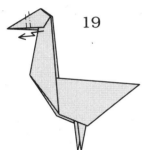

19

Fold the tip
in and out.

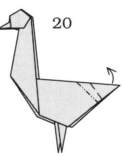

20

Fold the tail
in and out.

21

Fold behind,
repeat behind.

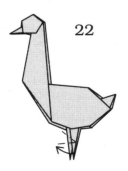

22

Bend to form
the feet.

23

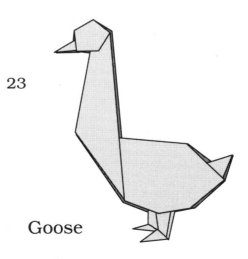

Goose

Flamingo

1

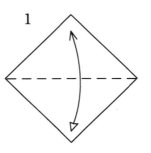

Fold and unfold.

2

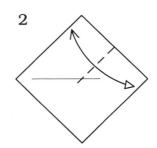

Fold one corner to
the other and unfold.

3

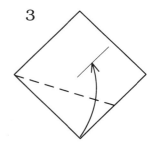

Fold the corner
to the center line.

4

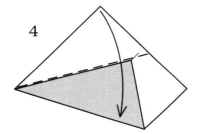

5

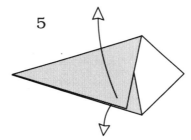

Unfold.

6

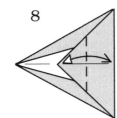

Fold to the creases.

7

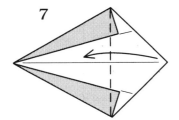

8

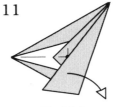

Fold and unfold.

9

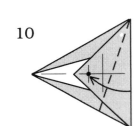

Fold and unfold.

10

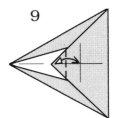

11

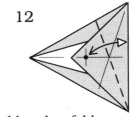

Unfold.

12

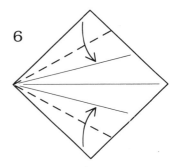

Fold and unfold.

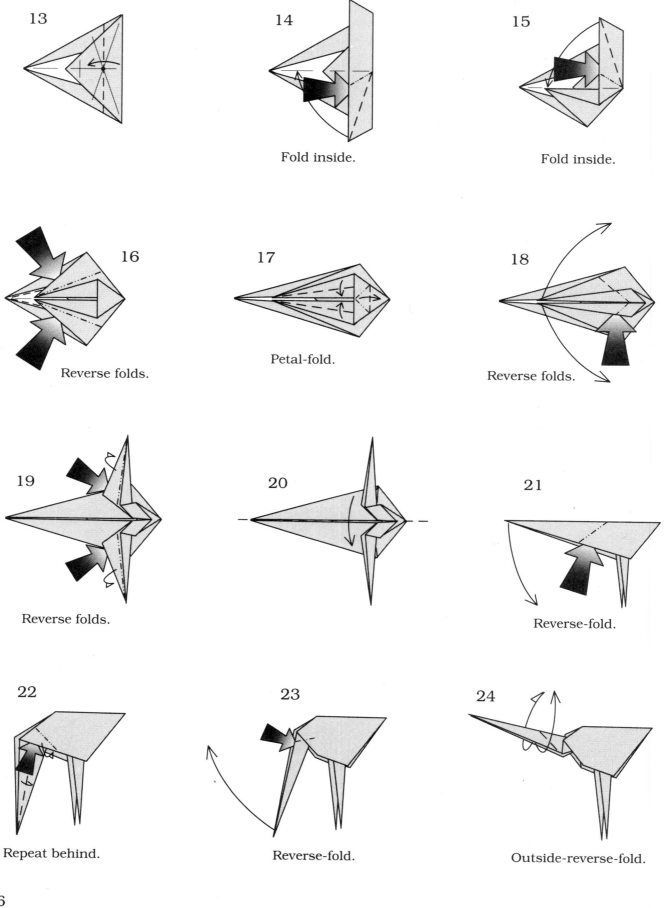

13

14

Fold inside.

15

Fold inside.

16

Reverse folds.

17

Petal-fold.

18

Reverse folds.

19

Reverse folds.

20

21

Reverse-fold.

22

Repeat behind.

23

Reverse-fold.

24

Outside-reverse-fold.

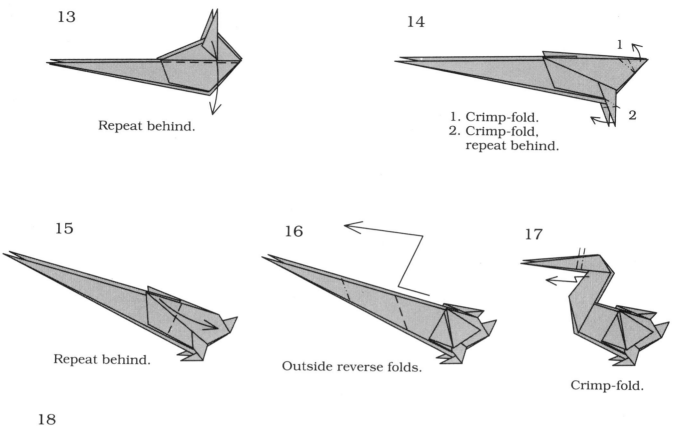

13

Repeat behind.

14

1
2

1. Crimp-fold.
2. Crimp-fold,
   repeat behind.

15

Repeat behind.

16

Outside reverse folds.

17

Crimp-fold.

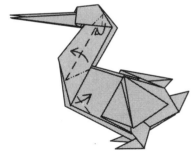

18

Repeat behind.

19

Open the beak.

20

Pelican

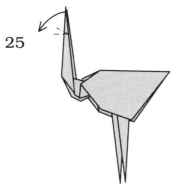

25

Spread the paper.

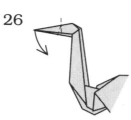

26

Spread the paper
while crimp folding.

27

Crimp-fold.

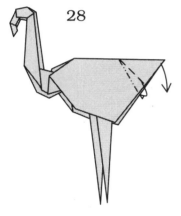

28

Crimp-fold.

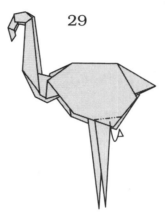

29

Fold behind,
repeat behind.

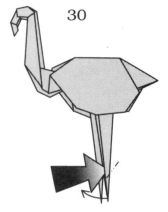

30

Reverse-fold,
repeat behind.

31

Squeeze the legs, the
flamingo can stand.

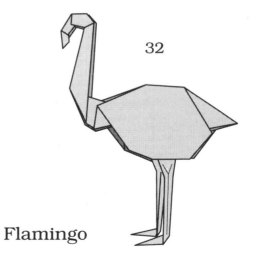

32

Flamingo

Pelican

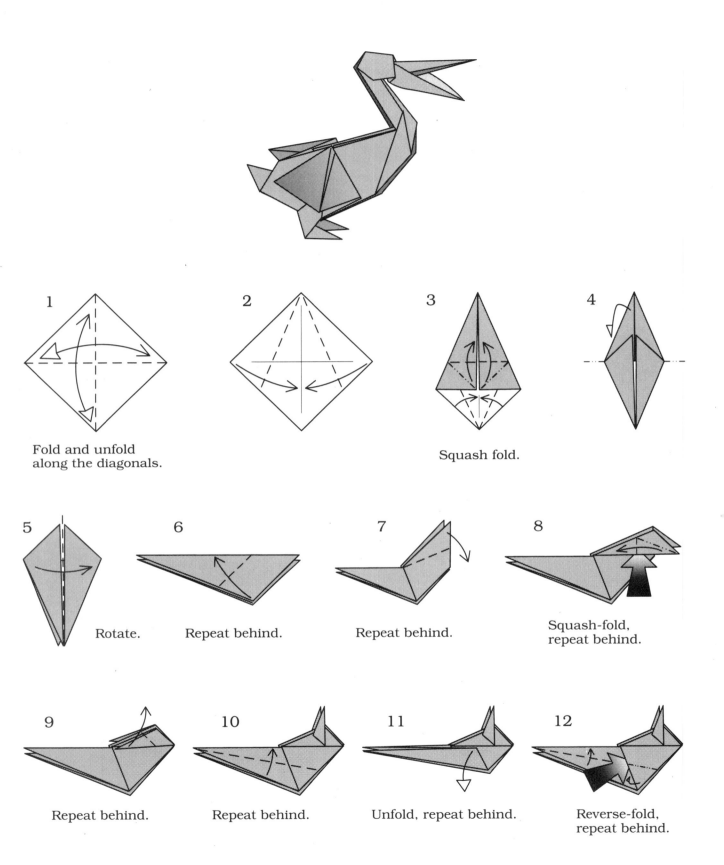

1

Fold and unfold
along the diagonals.

2

3

Squash fold.

4

5

Rotate.

6

Repeat behind.

7

Repeat behind.

8

Squash-fold,
repeat behind.

9

Repeat behind.

10

Repeat behind.

11

Unfold, repeat behind.

12

Reverse-fold,
repeat behind.

Heron

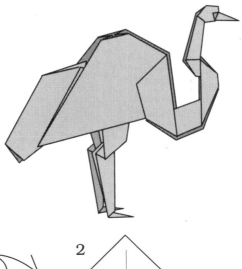

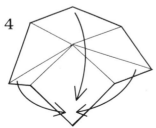

1

Fold and unfold along the diagonals.

2

Fold and unfold.

3

Collapse the square by bringing the four corners together.

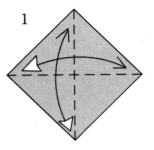

4

This is a three-dimensional intermediate step.

5

Kite-fold, repeat behind.

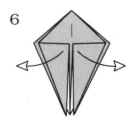

6

Unfold, repeat behind.

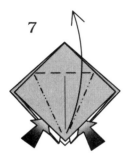

7

Petal-fold.

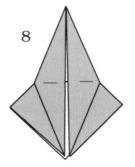

8

Repeat step 7 behind.

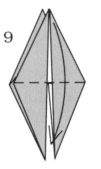

9

Repeat behind.

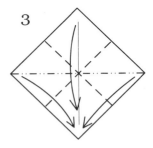

10

Repeat behind.

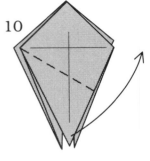

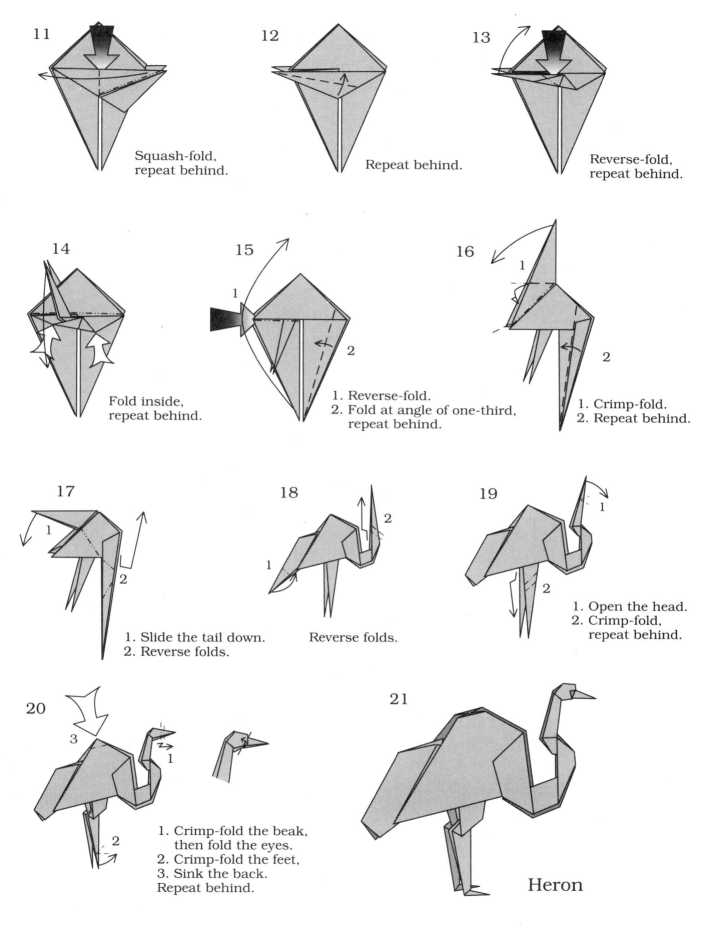

11

Squash-fold,
repeat behind.

12

Repeat behind.

13

Reverse-fold,
repeat behind.

14

Fold inside,
repeat behind.

15

1. Reverse-fold.
2. Fold at angle of one-third,
   repeat behind.

16

1. Crimp-fold.
2. Repeat behind.

17

1. Slide the tail down.
2. Reverse folds.

18

Reverse folds.

19

1. Open the head.
2. Crimp-fold,
   repeat behind.

20

1. Crimp-fold the beak,
   then fold the eyes.
2. Crimp-fold the feet,
3. Sink the back.
Repeat behind.

21

Heron

Pheasant

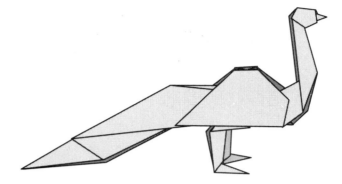

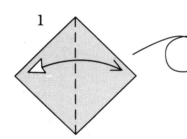

1

Fold and unfold.

2

Kite-fold.

3

Unfold.

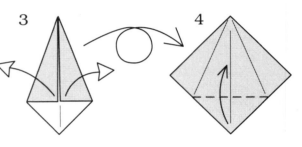

4

5

6

Unfold.

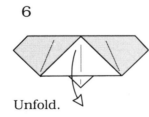

7

8

Squash-fold.

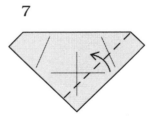

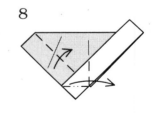

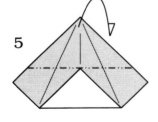

9

Squash-fold.

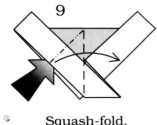

10

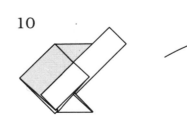

11

Squash-fold.

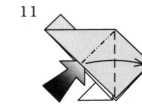

12

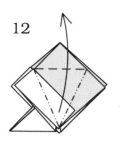

Petal-fold,
repeat behind.

13

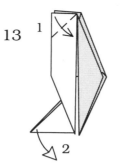

1. Repeat behind.
2. Pull out.

14

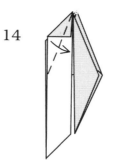

Repeat behind.

15

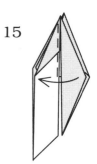

16

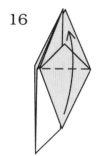

17

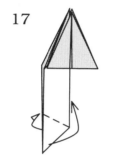

Outside-reverse-fold.

18

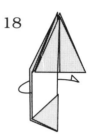

19

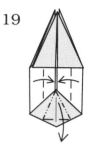

Petal-fold.

20

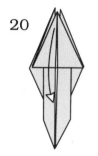

21

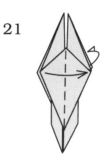

22

Repeat behind.

23

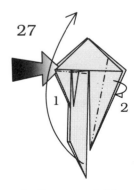

Rabbit-ear,
repeat behind.

24

Repeat behind.

25

Reverse-fold,
repeat behind.

26

Fold inside,
repeat behind.

27

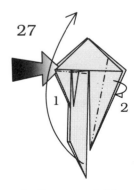

1. Reverse-fold.
2. Repeat behind.

28

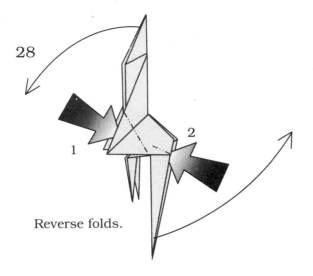

Reverse folds.

29

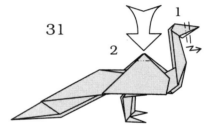

30

1. Spread the paper
   to form the head.
2. Crimp-fold,
   repeat behind.

31

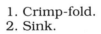

1. Crimp-fold.
2. Sink.

32

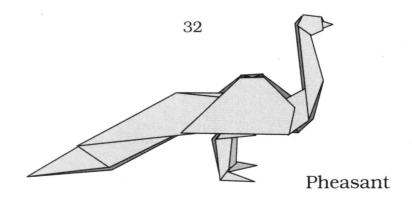

Pheasant

Seagull

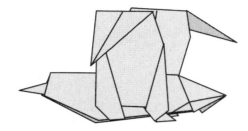

1

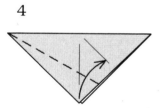

2

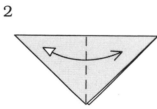

Fold and unfold.

3

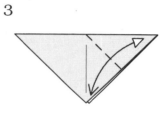

Fold and unfold.

4

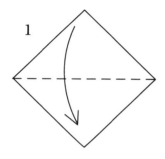

Fold the corner
to the line.

5

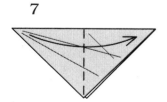

6

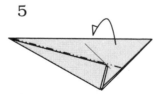

Unfold.

7

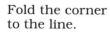

8

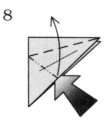

Squash-fold.

9

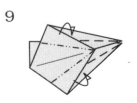

Reverse folds.

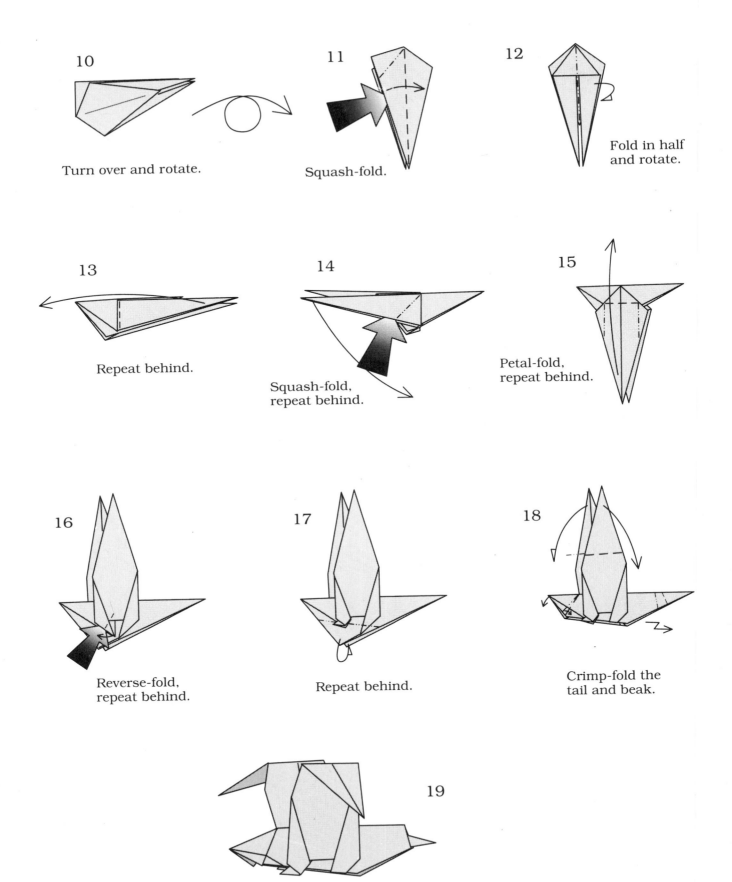

10

Turn over and rotate.

11

Squash-fold.

12

Fold in half
and rotate.

13

Repeat behind.

14

Squash-fold,
repeat behind.

15

Petal-fold,
repeat behind.

16

Reverse-fold,
repeat behind.

17

Repeat behind.

18

Crimp-fold the
tail and beak.

19

Seagull

Hummingbird

1

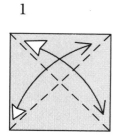

Fold and unfold
along the diagonals.

2

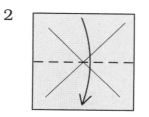

3

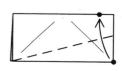

Fold the corner
to the top.

4

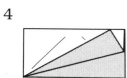

5

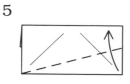

6

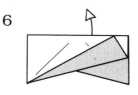

Open.

7

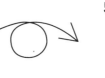

Squash folds.

8

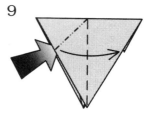

Fold in half and rotate.

9

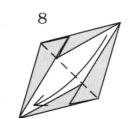

Squash-fold,
repeat behind.

10

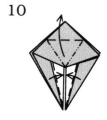

Petal-fold,
repeat behind.

11

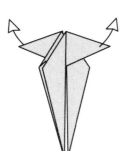

Pull out, repeat
behind.

12

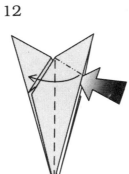
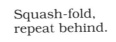

Squash-fold,
repeat behind.

13

Petal-fold.

14

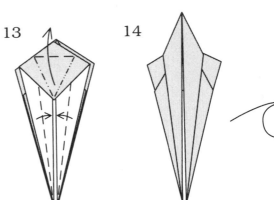

15

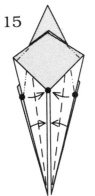

Bring the dots
together.

16

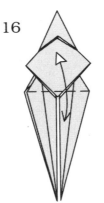

Fold and unfold.

17

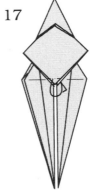

18

19

20

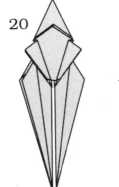

21

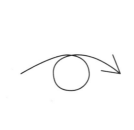

22

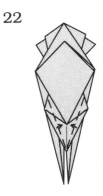
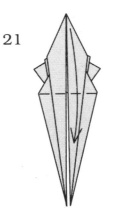

Fold at an angle
of one-third.

23

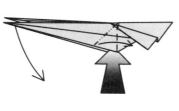

24

Squash-fold,
repeat behind.

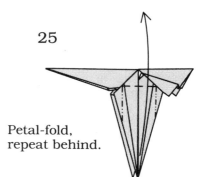

25

Petal-fold,
repeat behind.

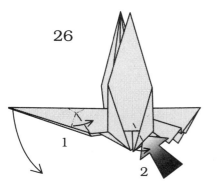

26

1. This is similar to a crimp fold.
2. Reverse-fold, repeat behind.

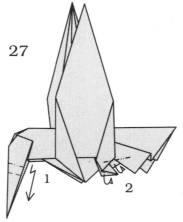

27

1. Crimp-fold.
2. Repeat behind.

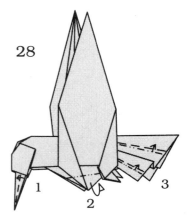

28

Repeat behind.

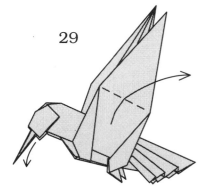

29

Repeat behind.

30

Hummingbird

Cardinal

1

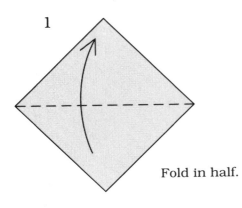

Fold in half.

2

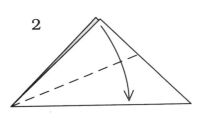

Fold one side down.

3

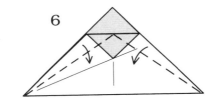

Unfold.

4

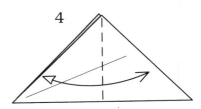

5

6

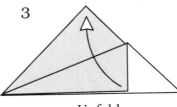

7

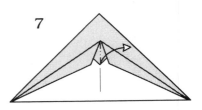

Pull out the corner.

8

9

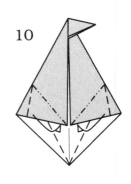

10

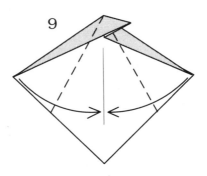

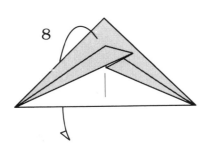

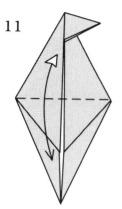 11

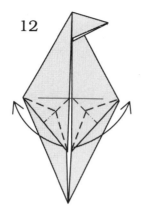 12

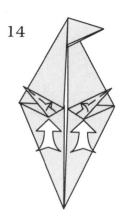 13

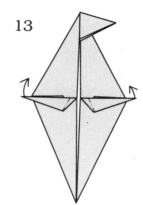 14

Fold down and unfold.

Rabbit ears.

Spread-squash-fold.

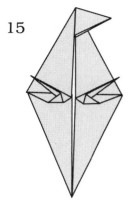 15

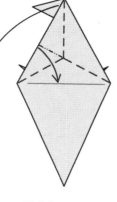 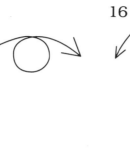 16

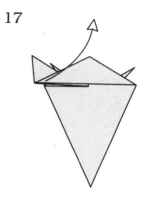 17

Rabbit-ear.

Unfold.

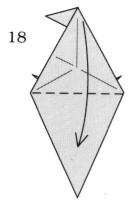 18

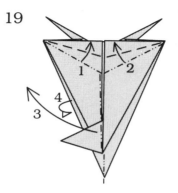 19

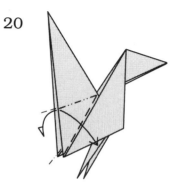 20

Crimp-fold.

21

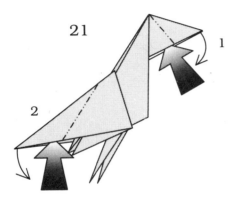

Reverse folds.

22

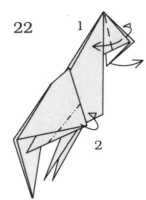

Repeat behind.

23

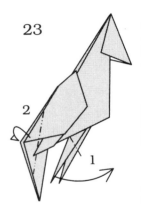

Repeat behind.

24

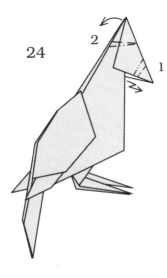

25

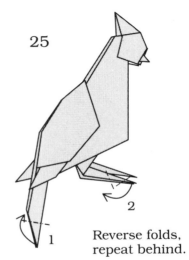

Reverse folds,
repeat behind.

26

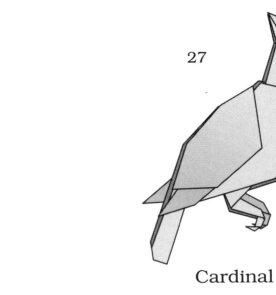

1. Sink.
2. Crimp-fold.

27

Cardinal

Cormorant

1

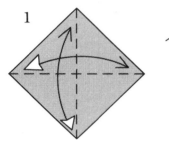

Fold and unfold
along the diagonals.

2

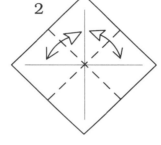

Fold and unfold.

3

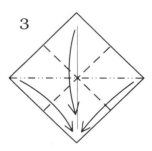

Collapse the square
by bringing the four
corners together.

4

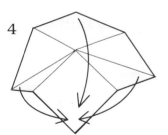

This is a three-
dimensional
intermediate step.

5

Kite-fold.

6

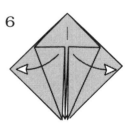

Unfold.

7

Reverse folds.

8

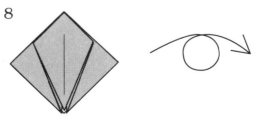

9

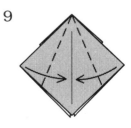

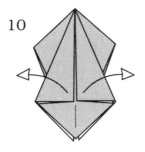

10

Unfold.

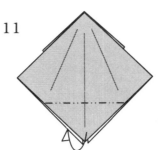

11

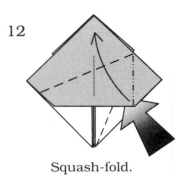

12

Squash-fold.

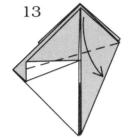

13

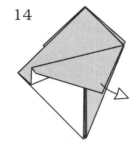

14

Unfold.

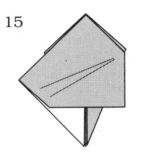

15

Repeat steps 12–14 on the left.

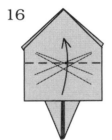

16

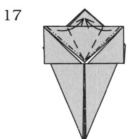

17

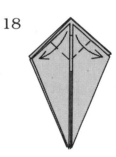

18

Squash-fold.

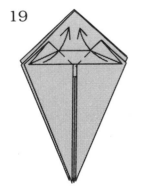

19

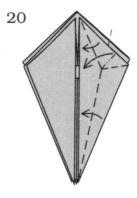

20

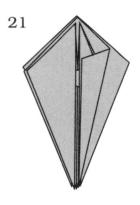

21

Repeat step 20 on the left.

22

Reverse folds.

23

24

25

26

1. Valley-fold, repeat behind.
2. Reverse-fold.

27

1. Outside-reverse-fold.
2. Crimp-fold.
3. Open the wings.

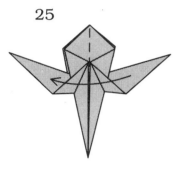

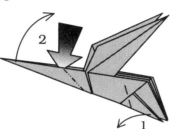

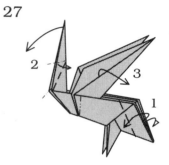

28

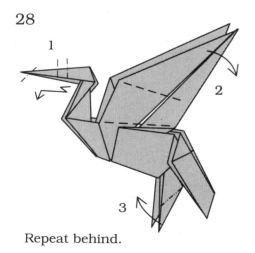

Repeat behind.

29

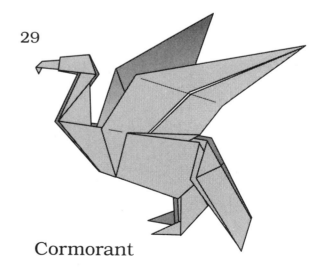

Cormorant

Stork

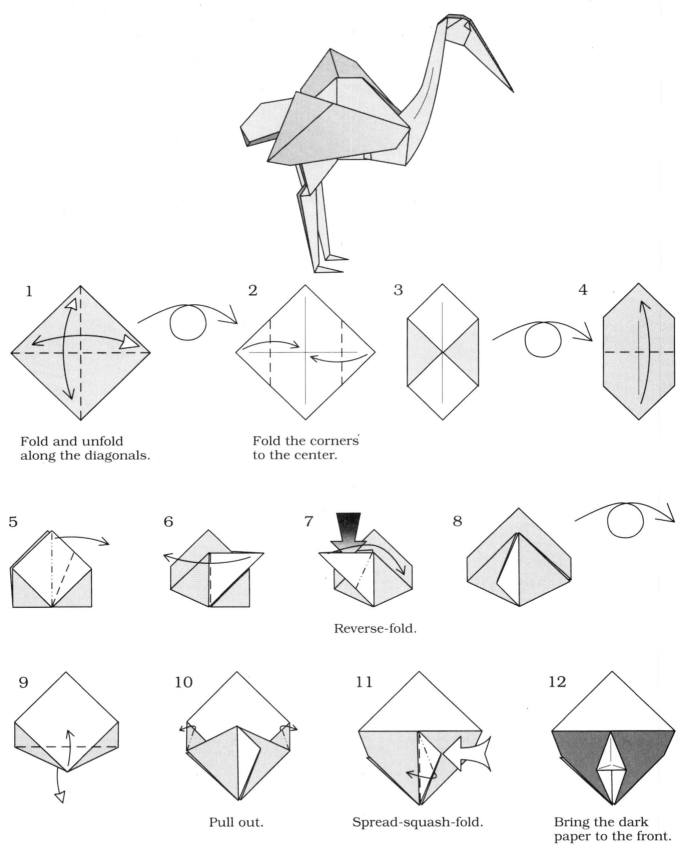

1

Fold and unfold
along the diagonals.

2

Fold the corners
to the center.

3

4

5

6

7

Reverse-fold.

8

9

10

Pull out.

11

Spread-squash-fold.

12

Bring the dark
paper to the front.

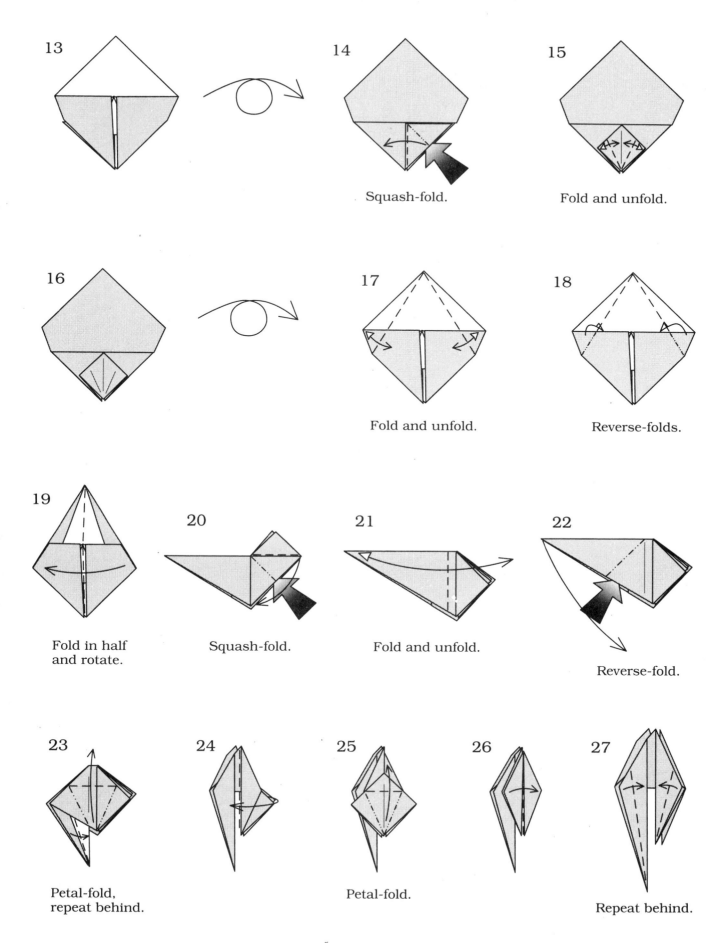

13

14

Squash-fold.

15

Fold and unfold.

16

17

Fold and unfold.

18

Reverse-folds.

19

Fold in half
and rotate.

20

Squash-fold.

21

Fold and unfold.

22

Reverse-fold.

23

Petal-fold,
repeat behind.

24

25

Petal-fold.

26

27

Repeat behind.

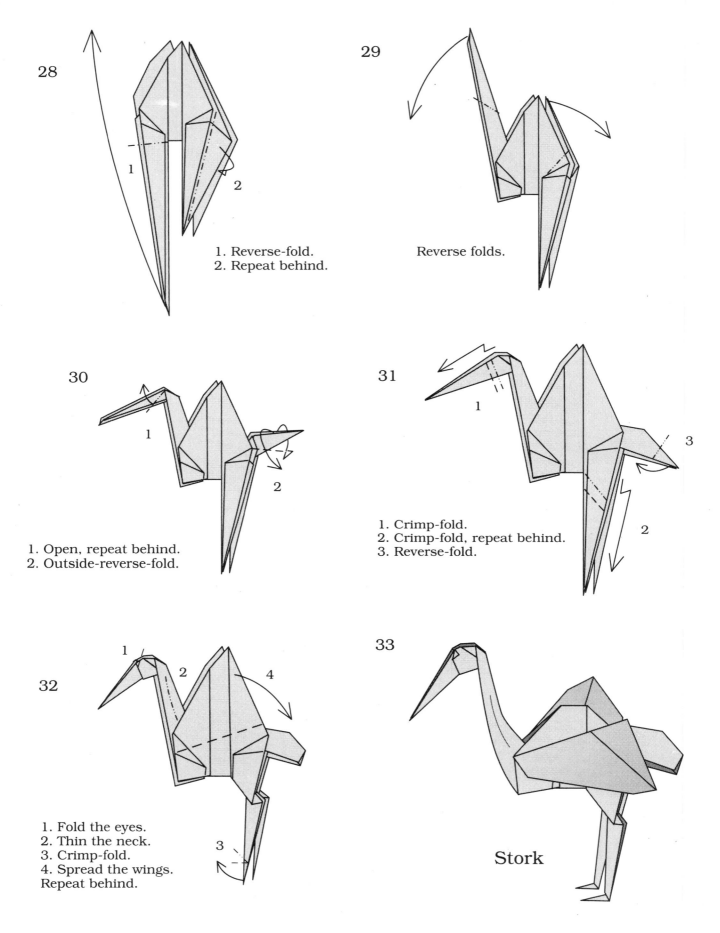

28

1. Reverse-fold.
2. Repeat behind.

29

Reverse folds.

30

1. Open, repeat behind.
2. Outside-reverse-fold.

31

1. Crimp-fold.
2. Crimp-fold, repeat behind.
3. Reverse-fold.

32

1. Fold the eyes.
2. Thin the neck.
3. Crimp-fold.
4. Spread the wings.
Repeat behind.

33

Stork

Eagle

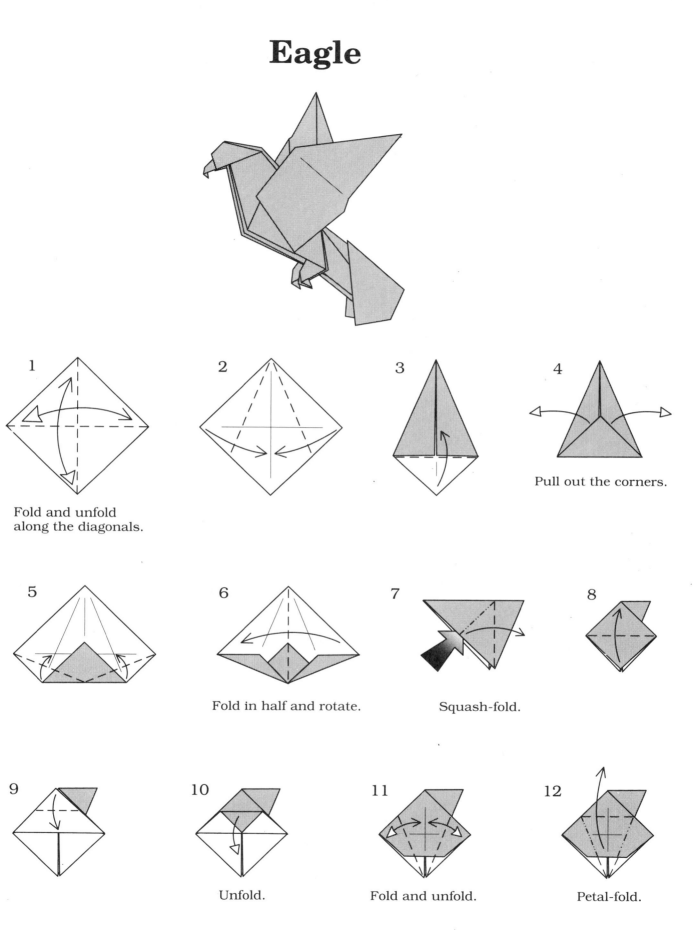

1 Fold and unfold along the diagonals.

2

3

4 Pull out the corners.

5

6 Fold in half and rotate.

7 Squash-fold.

8

9

10 Unfold.

11 Fold and unfold.

12 Petal-fold.

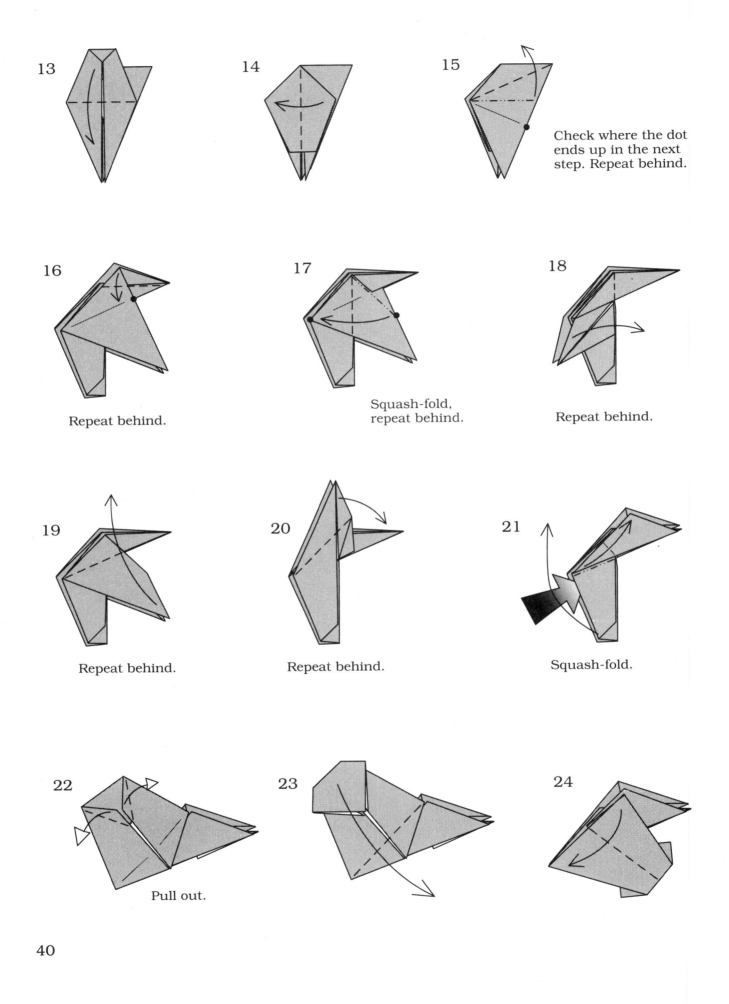

13

14

15 Check where the dot ends up in the next step. Repeat behind.

16 Repeat behind.

17 Squash-fold, repeat behind.

18 Repeat behind.

19 Repeat behind.

20 Repeat behind.

21 Squash-fold.

22 Pull out.

23

24

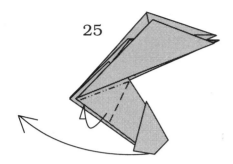

25

Crimp-fold.

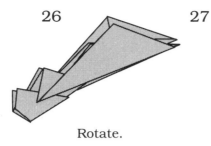

26

Rotate.

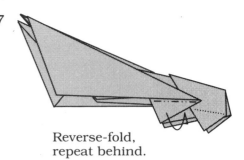

27

Reverse-fold,
repeat behind.

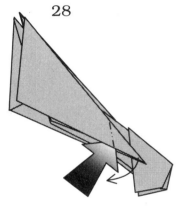

28

Reverse-fold,
repeat behind.

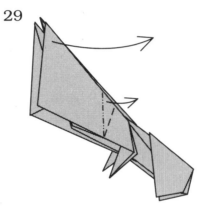

29

Squash-fold,
repeat behind.

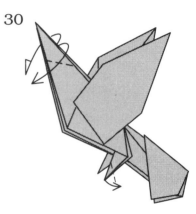

30

Outside-reverse-fold the
head. Reverse-fold the
feet, repeat behind.

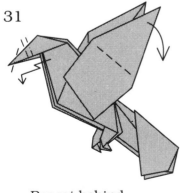

31

Repeat behind.

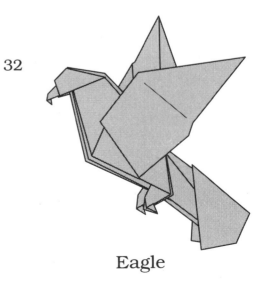

32

Eagle

Canary

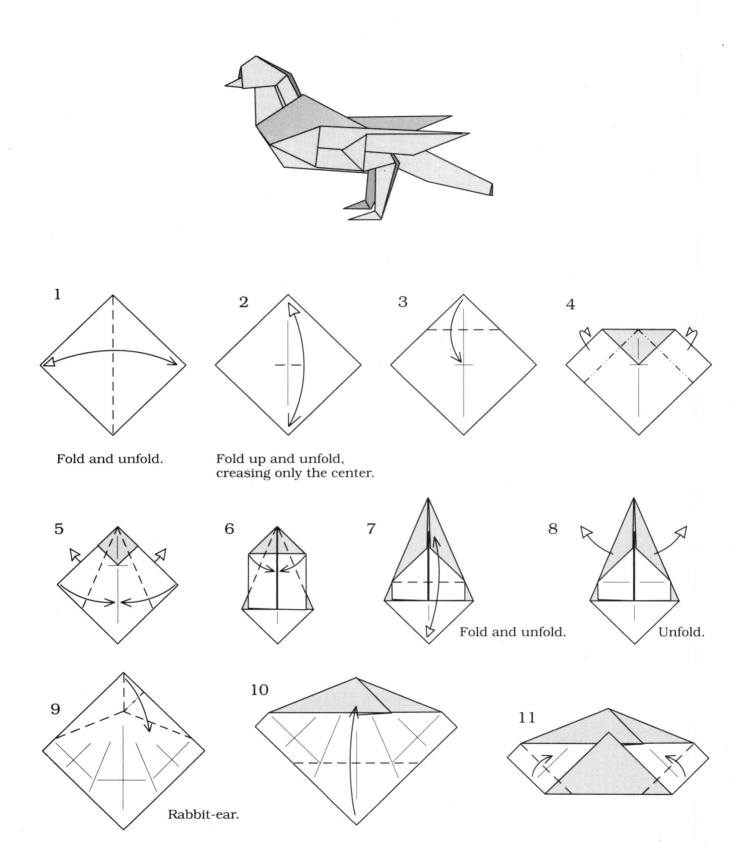

1

Fold and unfold.

2

Fold up and unfold,
creasing only the center.

3

4

5

6

7

Fold and unfold.

8

Unfold.

9

Rabbit-ear.

10

11

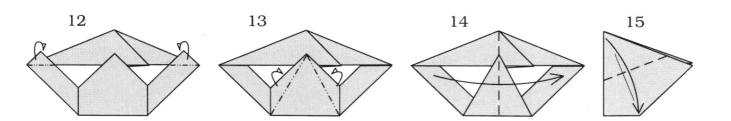

12

13

14

15

16

17

Unfold.

18

Pull out the
inside flap.

19

Repeat behind
and rotate.

20

21

Reverse folds.

22

Reverse-fold.

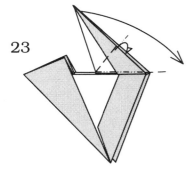

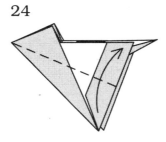

23

Crimp-fold.

24

Repeat behind.

25

Reverse-fold,
repeat behind.

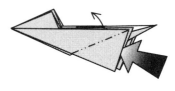

26

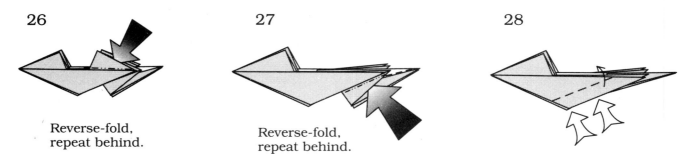

Reverse-fold,
repeat behind.

27

Reverse-fold,
repeat behind.

28

Spread-squash-fold the
wing, repeat behind.

29

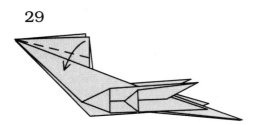

Fold at an angle of one-third,
repeat behind.

30

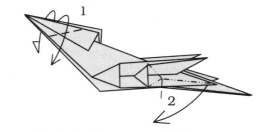

1. Outside-reverse-fold.
2. Double-rabbit-ear,
   repeat behind.

31

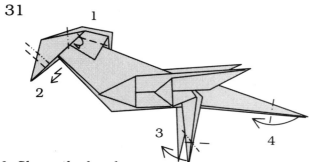

1. Shape the head.
2. Form the beak.
3. Shape the foot.
4. Reverse-fold the tail.
Repeat behind.

32

1. Crimp-fold.
2. Repeat behind.

33

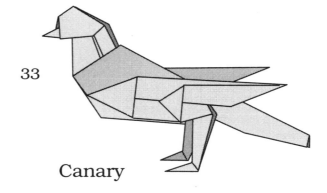

Canary

Parrot

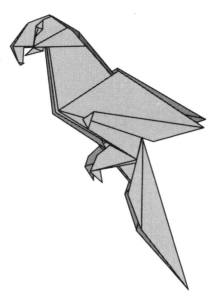

1

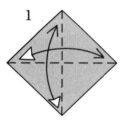

Fold and unfold
along the diagonals.

2

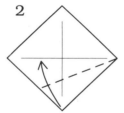

Crease lightly.

3

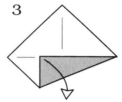

Unfold.

4

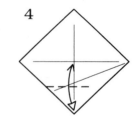

Fold up to the center
and unfold. Crease
lightly and only on
the left side.

5

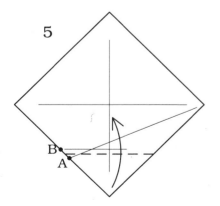

Fold up so that A meets the
line above it, close to B.

6

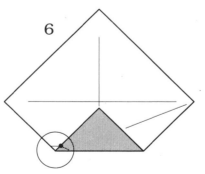

Note how the
creases intersect
inside the circle.

7

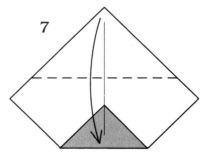

8

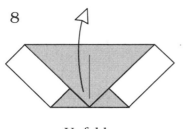

Unfold.

9

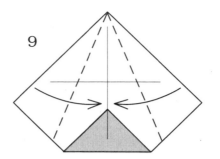

10

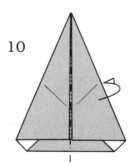

Fold in half
and rotate.

11

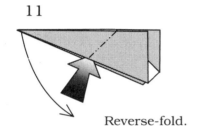

Reverse-fold.

12

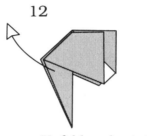

Unfold and rotate.

13

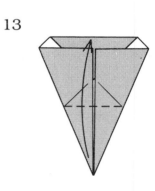

14

15

16

17

Tuck inside and rotate.

18

Rabbit-ear.

19

Squash-fold.

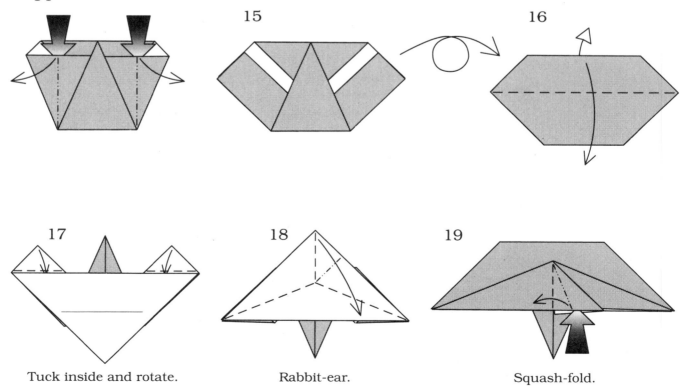

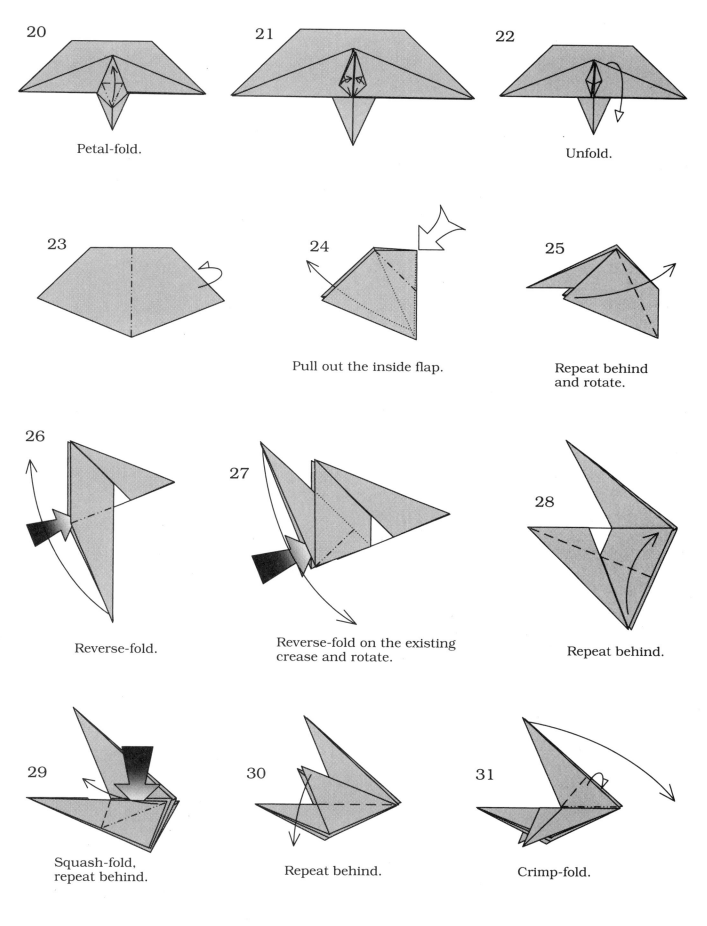

20 Petal-fold.

21

22 Unfold.

23

24 Pull out the inside flap.

25 Repeat behind and rotate.

26 Reverse-fold.

27 Reverse-fold on the existing crease and rotate.

28 Repeat behind.

29 Squash-fold, repeat behind.

30 Repeat behind.

31 Crimp-fold.

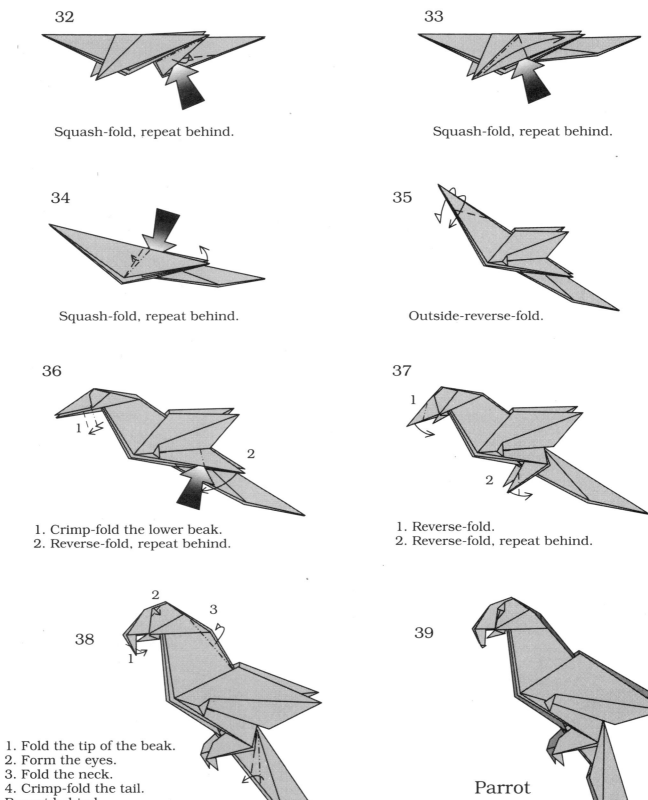

32

Squash-fold, repeat behind.

33

Squash-fold, repeat behind.

34

Squash-fold, repeat behind.

35

Outside-reverse-fold.

36

1. Crimp-fold the lower beak.
2. Reverse-fold, repeat behind.

37

1. Reverse-fold.
2. Reverse-fold, repeat behind.

38

1. Fold the tip of the beak.
2. Form the eyes.
3. Fold the neck.
4. Crimp-fold the tail.
Repeat behind.

39

Parrot